To Courtney
With love
Grandpa Jack + Mimi W.
1982

Nature Library of Color

BABY AND SMALL ANIMALS

CRESCENT

A baby animal, frolicking in the field or wrestling furiously with its littermates is one of the few sights in this world that wins universal affection. The familiar cooing noises that we make with our own young are elicited from us by almost any infant, and a nestful of tiny balls of fluff, which is how so many animals are for the early part of their life, warms even the coldest of hearts. Some baby animals appeal more to us than others – no doubt every animal is attracted to young who resemble more closely their own – perhaps this is why we find kittens and baby owls, with their big, round eyes set close together in a short face with a high-rounded forehead, so irresistible. But we also like animals that mimic us, such as monkeys, and penguins that walk upright, and even the babies of hoofed animals still evoke in us tender feelings as they attempt to steady themselves on those long, gangly legs and totter inquisitively towards an outstretched hand to enjoy a morsel of food or a stroke. There are numerous wild animals who live far away from man's urbanised world, who are ferocious, and who, in adulthood, do not endear themselves to us at all, either to look at or in the way they live – the wild boar is one such creature. But their babies display the same charming qualities that win us over, albeit for a short period of time.

This book is concerned with the young of animals and also many of the smaller mammals who remain as delightful to look at in adulthood as when they are babies. Mammals are set apart from the rest of the animal kingdom. Their name comes from the fact that they feed their young on milk produced in the mammary glands and they are warm blooded and consequently suited to a variety of climates. They range enormously in size and shape; the smallest – some of the rodents weigh as little as a fraction of an ounce when fully grown; and the largest – some of the whales weigh about fifty million times as much. The whale's true size is only really appreciated by us when

Most young puppies are absolutely adorable, and these are no exception. (1),(2) and (5) show a proud Golden Retriever with her delightful pups. The same pups are shown on their own (3). Young Cocker Spaniels have snub noses and domed foreheads (4), while Welsh Corgi pups (6) are extremely fluffy!

1

2

5

6

1

2

3

5

4

6

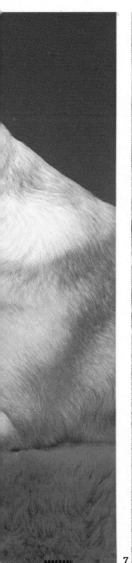

it is removed from its natural, aquatic home and shown in relation to an object we are well aquainted with. Yet these and the many millions of species in between share essential features which belong to the mammal group, particularly relating to the rearing of their young.

Surprisingly, mammals originated from reptiles, a fact which is clearly evident in the reproductive processes of the most primitive of living mammals, the monotremes, which include the duck-billed platypus and spiny ant-eaters of Australia, as well as in the slightly more advanced pouched mammals known collectively as marsupials. Who would believe that a five foot kangaroo is at birth only an inch long? An egg is 'laid' and retained inside the body until the embryo has used up all the nourishment contained in the egg-yolk, which takes just forty days for the largest kangaroos. The baby is then born, but it is only very basically developed. It will spend the following six to eight months of its life fastened securely onto a teat in the pouch, to which it has crawled, unaided by its mother, and from which it eventually emerges, no longer an infant. The more advanced species of mammals, which make up a far greater proportion of the total population,

(1) Cocker Spaniel puppy; (2) Welsh Corgi pups; (3) Old English Sheepdog pup; (4) Golden Labrador pup; (5) Golden Labrador and Cocker Spaniel pup;

(6) Corgi pups; (7) Rough Collie pups; (8) English Setter puppies; (9) Basenji puppies.

have placentas where the embryo remains during development. Food is carried to it by the mother in her blood, the supply being therefore inexhaustible, and the baby (or babies) is born fairly well developed, although the stage of development varies from creature to creature. The mother can usually continue her normal life right up until the young are born.

The number of babies born at one time varies. In general, the smaller mammals, with relatively short lives, make nests and give birth to several infants, sometimes more than once or twice a year. These babies are born at an early stage of development and for the first few days, weeks or even months stay in the nest while their ears and eyes open. Constant attention from their mother is of vital importance. The life style that each animal is adapted for often provides a key as to whether the babies will be born at a late or early stage of development. Young rabbits, adapted to be born in a safe burrow, arrive after thirty-one days gestation and are blind and naked at birth. Hares, on the other hand, live a more hazardous existence. It is important that their young can move around quickly after birth and so they are born after about thirty-nine days gestation and at birth are fully furred and able to see.

The life expectancy of larger mammals is longer and many of them are adapted to a nomadic existence in their constant search for food. This is reflected in the number of children they bear at one time and the stage of development at which they are born. The African elephant carries its child in the womb for about twenty-two months before giving birth and more than one child at a time is very rare indeed. Many hoofed animals do give birth to twins but, as with humans, this is also uncommon.

Suckling

The baby mammal is dependent for its survival on its mother's milk. This vital food is produced in the mother's body at the time of birth and is transmitted in the most hygienic method through the mammary gland or teat straight into the baby's mouth. Mammals' milk contains energy-giving ingredients in the form of fats and

Previous page *Long-haired tabby kittens.* (1) *Kitten with Golden Labrador;* (2) *Retriever pup with kitten;* (3) *Cocker Spaniel puppies;* (4) *Labrador with long-haired blue-cream kitten;* (5) *Retriever pup and kitten;* (6) *Highland Terrier pup and kitten;* (7) *Springer Spaniel pups;* (8) *Cocker Spaniel pup.*

6

7

8

sugar, proteins for growth and vitamins and minerals essential to the health and vitality of the new-born baby.

With all baby mammals the act of suckling is instinctive. Within a few seconds of birth, although some are blind and helpless, all know how to locate their mothers' teats and how to go about suckling. This is done by moving their heads from side to side and performing nuzzling and sucking actions with their mouths. The mother in turn, accommodates her movements and positions to the baby's actions to facilitate the search. Once located, the young one's mouth clamps on to the nipple and automatically begins to suckle. It stimulates the flow of milk by prodding with its nose and 'treading' the surrounding swollen area around the nipple with its paws so that the milk is expressed freely. The suckling activity is intensely pleasurable for both the mother and the baby animal. The mammary glands are formed from sweat glands which, at the time of birth, adapt themselves to extract all the essential nutrients that are present in milk from the blood in the skin capillaries. The milk flows to the nipples through ducts formed by the joining of the glands. The number of teats present depends upon the size of the litter. Generally the placing of the teats can be found between the front legs or alternatively between the hind legs.

The process of weaning the baby from pure fluid to solid food is a gradual one, mainly because of the immunity factor. Initially the first fluid passes through the stomach wall of the baby straight into the blood stream. This first stage milk is called the colostrum and is vital not only because it contains the essential foods but because it carries the antibodies from the mother's blood necessary for protecting the baby from diseases. Introduction to solid food has to be a slow process to ensure that the baby has time to build up its own antibodies and is not totally dependent upon its mother's milk for immunity.

Tiny kittens are always so appealing, like (1) the blue shorthair; (2) black and white shorthair; (3) blue-cream shorthair; (4) and (7) white shorthair; (5) tabby and white shorthair; (6) marmalade shorthair and cream longhair; (8) white shorthair and tabby and white shorthair. More beautiful kittens appear on the next page.

6

8

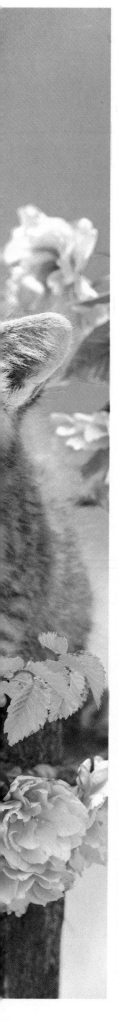

Most mammals suckle their young on land, though there are some truly aquatic mammals who do feed their young in the water, in which case the mammary glands are adapted to squirt milk into the babies' mouths. Whales and sometimes hippopotamuses are examples of such species. Other aquatic mammals come to shore to feed their babies and only return to the water when the young are old enough to fend for themselves.

The act of suckling is believed by psychologists to be all-important in the formation of a secure bond between mother and child, the close physical contact and mutual pleasure derived by both being crucial factors.

Partly because breastfeeding is regarded by some as an antisocial activity and also because of the inconvenience to some mothers who cannot or do not wish to be on call twenty-four hours a day, humans have developed a milk substitute which has proved an adequate replacement for mother's milk in terms of food value. If it is ever necessary to bring up an orphaned baby animal in the home, this milk will suffice. The advantages are that it can be stored and mixed, and administered by bottle by anyone.

Early Days

Baby mammals, however advanced they are just after birth, are never far from their mothers during the early days and even weeks of their lives. For the majority of them, 'Mum' is far more than just a milk machine.

Essential skills are required as an adult, as well as the basics of what to eat and how to obtain it, and these are learnt by copying her in everything she does. Those born in a nest, often naked and totally helpless need her to keep them warm and safe from outside dangers. Growing up is an exciting time, but it is often very dangerous and it takes time to become fully equipped for the adult world.

In these early days, nearly all the babies of small and hunting mammals are going to need carrying. Grazing animals can usually walk within an hour of being born, which is an adaptation to their nomadic lifestyle – a giraffe can stand within a matter of minutes after birth and can probably run faster than its mother by the time it is two weeks old. Some animals are carried even though they are well able to move speedily without help; animals who live in trees for instance, who develop sure limbs very quickly. However, carrying continues to take place because they still need the security of their mothers' warm bodies. Koalas like to cling to their mothers' backs, baboons and chimps hang on to the soft fur of the parent's belly. During the early climbing days babies are less adventurous, allowing their mothers to do most of the moving, but very soon, as they develop in strength and confidence, they begin to perfect circus-like tricks. Monkeys will move from the clinging underside position to bare-back riding while the parent is moving quite fast. Chimpanzees enjoy being carried on their mothers' backs for up to four years and would continue were it not for the parents who usually discourage them, especially if the mother is already carrying another infant. Nest babies will remain in the nest if it continues to provide a safe hiding place. But in the wild, tiny babies make perfect prey for a variety of larger animals and birds, so the mother keeps a watchful guard and is away from them as little as possible. If danger is imminent the mother will not fail to move her babies to a safer place. The mode of carrying the young varies with different species. Rodents seize the first part of the body that comes to the mouth while carnivore mothers usually carry their babies by the

(1) Long-haired white kitten; (2), (4) and (5) long-haired tabby and white kittens; (3) short-haired tabby and white kitten.

scruff of the neck. When the young become distressed they utter calls which in rodents may be on a frequency higher than the human ear can pick up, and the mother comes immediately to the rescue. Later, when they have learnt to walk, their behaviour changes and a warning call from their mother sends them running quickly from the nest to find their own hiding places.

As with all animals, a bond between mother and baby must be established quickly. The amount of time each mammal spends bringing up and taking care of its children varies enormously and it is not easy to establish which mothers become emotionally attached to their young and which are merely fulfilling a basic reproductive process. One similarity that does exist, from the

primates who care for their children for many years to the prolific rodents who abandon their babies shortly after birth, is that the mother will be fiercely protective for whatever length of time is naturally required for the young to become independent. A strong bond, whether instinctive or otherwise is formed. Parent-child bonds must be made

(1) and (2) White long-haired kittens; (3) long-haired blue tabby kitten; (4) and (7) a very curious short-haired blue tabby kitten, with a very disinterested mallard duckling! (5) Blue tabby longhair; (6) short-haired tabby and short-haired tabby and white kittens.

1

2

3

4

5

instantly after birth. There is no evidence to suggest that babies instinctively know their mothers; this occurs by recognising personal scent, shape and colour and is strengthened by the suckling process. Babies that are born at a late stage of development must play an active role in establishing this relationship, following the mother wherever she roams. Walrus babies grip their mother's back with their flippers and a young elephant often holds on to its mother's tail with its trunk. In the nest, the bond cannot fail to be established because the babies do not venture out for quite a while and the mother will be their only contact throughout this time. Family life rarely exists as we know it in the animal kingdom. The mother feeds and protects her babies, even actively driving the father away. But some mammals do co-operate with each other in rearing their young. When a female elephant leaves the main herd to give birth she is accompanied by one or two other females, known as 'aunties' who help with the birth and later with the protection of the young elephant. African Cape hunting dogs rear all their young in a communal burrow. All the females may nurse all the pups, regardless of which baby belongs to which mother. When the pack goes out hunting, several females and a few males stay behind to care for the young. Cousins can be as useful as aunties. In a monkey group young females will often stay close to a mother with a baby and take great delight in fondling and grooming it. This is advantageous because if the mother is injured and cannot look after her baby, others will be able to take on the role.

Sooner or later, usually when the mother is ready to have another baby, it is time for the young to fend for themselves and they will either be driven away, or the mother will leave home.

Baby Household Pets – Breeding

All mammals, with the possible exception of the sophisticated human being, are naturals when it comes to breeding and taking care of their young. In this respect household pets are no exception to the rule. One of

Downy goslings (1), (4) and (6) look bright and alert, while even at an early age the muscovy ducklings are clearly defined (2). An Aylesbury duck keeps a careful eye on her ducklings (5) and these chicks (3) and (7) are just bundles of fluff.

the great delights of humans, for whom animals form an integral part of family life, is being around when their pets give birth, to observe them taking care of their young and to watch the enchanting antics of the tiny pets as they are growing up. It is always touching to see the way in which female pets instinctively know how to be perfect mothers, and the trust and devotion shown to them by the young ones. There is very little a pet owner has to do when it comes to breeding time, other than to provide a warm ambience, adequate food, peace and quiet and the minimum of interference.

Cats, one of the most popular and loved of household pets are most independent and efficient when it comes to breeding. Apart from

certain pure feline breeds which are more highly strung and do not always take to motherhood with total ease, the majority of cats rarely present any problem to their owners. It can be that over-excitable owners present difficulties for their cats, so care should be taken not to interfere with the natural processes which the animal instinctively knows how to deal with or it may become extremely nervous and lose its milk. Cats usually come on heat between the ages of six months and a year. This happens at regular intervals of six months, so unless they are speyed, females can give birth to two litters a year for several years. During the gestation period, which takes from fifty-eight to seventy days, it is necessary to feed

Cygnets, ducklings and chicks are so appealing, with their tiny bodies covered in feathery down and their bright eyes intent on what goes on around them.

1

2

3

5

a cat almost twice the amount of food it normally eats and to provide a nest box where it can feel safe, warm and undisturbed. When the birth takes place, often in strange places like shoeboxes or behind cupboards (usually somewhere that the cat has worked out in advance but which always comes as a surprise to the other members of the household), the cat will perform all the functions of an experienced midwife, including the disposal of the afterbirth. The cleanliness of this animal is remarkable. The place where the birth has occurred will be immaculate and she will be found reclining contentedly with half a dozen sleek kittens suckling at her teats. It is normal for a cat to give birth to a litter of four to six kittens. Occasionally one of the kittens may be a runt; that means it will be the weakling of the litter. In this case, instinct will tell the mother to let it die. This is often distressing to the owners who may even try to encourage the cat to take more care of the kitten – a useless exercise as cats know best about these matters and will be adamant in their rejection of runts. During the first weeks the mother cat will take devoted care of all her kittens' needs, nursing them, cleaning them, playing with them. Because she is suckling her litter she will require extra feeding. At birth the kittens are deaf, blind and virtually helpless. They will spend three-quarters of their time asleep in a communal huddle and the rest of the time suckling, apart from scrambling around like a game of mucical chairs to find a teat. After about ten days their eyes open and they begin to turn into little fluffy balls. Kittens' first teeth appear after a month. At this time they begin to behave mischievously and their antics are hilarious to watch. At eight weeks they should be fully weaned, by which time they are ready to leave the litter. It is preferable if one of the kittens can be kept for the mother, so as not to deprive her of her whole litter, but this is not always possible. The rest are usually given away to begin their lifetime of feline domination over another family.

(1) and (4) Budgerigars; (2) tawny owl; (3) young owls; (5) blue tit with family; (6) robin with young; (7) hedge-sparrow acts as foster parent to young cuckoo.

When the household pet happens to be a dog, the members of the household are much more involved, in the sense that "man's best friend" is much more dependent on human contact during the pregnancy period than a cat is. The owners have to take more care to do the right things both before and after the birth of the puppies. The female dog reaches sexual maturity at around eight or nine months of age. Unlike the cat, however, the period of gestation is more exact. The time of mating to the actual birth of the litter usually takes sixty-three days. It is advisable quite early on in the pregnancy for the owners to decide on the best place for the birth and the ensuing nursing period, so as to get the bitch acclimatised to her surroundings well

before the event. In this way the dog will feel secure and be able to develop her maternal instincts to the full. The birth is usually straight-forward, but it is as well for the owners to check discreetly that all is running smoothly in case a vet has to be consulted. During the first weeks the mother must be left to care for her puppies undisturbed as the demands made by her pups will be heavy and she may be distracted from her maternal function and become irritable with her puppies. If she needs human contact with members of the household as is sometimes the case, then she will leave her litter and seek it herself. Puppies, like cats, are also born blind. Their eyes open after about twelve days and they begin to hear soon after. Slightly later their teeth

Guinea pigs, tame mice and hamsters make delightful pets, being easy to keep and fairly undemanding. Their size, also, is not too intimidating for young children. Other rodents, like squirrels, are far too independent generally to be kept as pets, although they never fail to charm when seen in their natural habitat.

1

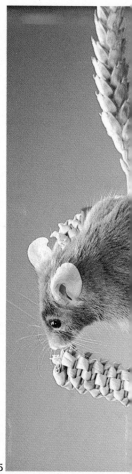

2

3

4

5

6

develop and they can crawl about and stand up. At three months puppies are at their most delightful. They scamper about, driving their patient mother to distraction. They are extremely mischievous, soft and lovable and everybody who comes into contact with them is totally captivated. Puppies make the most rewarding pets, but do require an enormous amount of care and attention if they are to become happy and healthy dogs.

Although also requiring care and attention, rabbits are much easier to keep than dogs. They make excellent pets for children, providing it is the child who does the looking after and not the mother! Breeding baby bunnies should be no problem to the owners since rabbits breed prolifically – underpopulation will never be a problem for this species! The rabbit generally makes a good mother. There is the occasional danger that a rabbit, when disturbed, will become worried and eat its young, so it is essential to take no risks and to leave this animal alone for three or four days before and after the birth. The normal gestation period for a doe is about thirty-one days. As with the other pets, rabbits need more food during their pregnancy; nearly twice as much as they normally receive. During the nursing period the mother will eat about three times as much as usual. The numbers of babies in a litter will vary enormously, from as few as two to as many as eighteen, though a litter of half a dozen is most common. Baby rabbits are born blind and are covered only by a gossamer-fine layer of down, but by ten days the eyes are open and at four weeks they are fully formed. Weaning takes place at this time and when they are three months old the young rabbits are ready to inhabit hutches of their own and should be moved. Rabbits form attachments to humans. It is not unknown to find rabbits who have the freedom of the house. But these bunnies think they are dogs! Rabbits can be nervous creatures, especially if children are particularly noisy or if they are handled roughly, and they can develop an aversion to people who are not rabbit-trained. The latter have to watch out for nipped fingers as rabbits have razor sharp teeth.

(1) Syrian hamster; (2) dormouse with young; (3) golden hamster; (4) and (5) an extremely agile brown mouse; (6) golden cavy (Guinea pig); (7) squirrel; (8) albino cavy; (9) hamster.

Rodents make ideal pets because they are easy and inexpensive to keep. They are great favourites with children who delight in handling them. The ones most commonly kept as pets are mice, rats, gerbils, hamsters and Guinea pigs.

Breeding rodents presents difficulties only in so far as they are exceptionally prolific. Mice, for instance, can create a population explosion in a very short space of time. The babies are born after a gestation period of only twenty days and they enter the world blind, deaf and totally naked, without even a vestige of down on their bodies, which are dark pink in colour. Within a couple of days however, a profusion of silky fur has formed and after two-and-a-half weeks they are well-furred, their beady alert eyes are fully opened and they are actively experimenting away from their nests. Five weeks after weaning they are on the reproduction circuit themselves. Since each female can carry a litter of half a dozen at a time about ten times a year, a pet owner can start up a thriving mouse business in a very short time.

However, not all pet rodents reproduce at the same rate. The Guinea pig for instance, may have trouble at the mating stage because the male can be so savage that putting them together in a cage is not always possible. Once Guinea pigs have chosen their mates though, they are one of the very rare species who stay together for the rest of their lives. When the Guinea pig is with young it carries its babies, usually a litter of two to six, for sixty-eight days. This long gestation period means that the babies are very well developed when they are born. Their eyes are wide open, they are fully furred and can even groom themselves straight away. Within a day these confident little animals can nibble at solids. Because Guinea pigs do not start breeding until they are two months old and have a long gestation period their rate of reproduction is not considered high in the rodent world.

(1) and (6) Orange Rex rabbit; (2) and (5) white rabbit; (3), (4) and (7) Dutch rabbits—these are complicated and difficult to breed, as the markings should be clear-cut and symmetrical. (8) Two cuddly grey rabbits pose among the primroses.

7

8

Zoo Babies

People everywhere in the world love zoos, especially in spring and summer when the majority of the animal population give birth to their young. A visit to the zoo can be a real education at this time, if one is interested in the study of parent-child behaviour of mammals. Certain events make the newspapers, like the birth of babies of such species as the panda or the polar bear. These are rare events and when they occur they generate great interest and queues form as visitors flock in droves to witness and photograph the young animal stars.

Everybody loves watching young animals especially when they have reached the stage where they perform and frolic mischievously in front of the crowd. Not all babies are in evidence though. Some animal mothers shun the crowds and exhibit neurotic symptons so they have to be removed from view in the interests of their babies.

The monkey house is rarely without serveral pairs of mothers and offspring of various types. They are unfailingly a delight to watch because they are extrovert creatures and exhibit their maternal talents without a trace of inhibition in front of the crowd. Monkeys are wonderfully protective mothers, cradling and grooming their young endlessly and forever displaying them proudly to the crowd. Their agility is breath-taking. It is not uncommon to see a female monkey, complete with baby clinging and suckling at its belly, suddenly rise from a squatting position, spring to a phenomenal height in one leap and swing right across the cage to a distant branch, without so much as displacing the baby's body from its original position. Although baby monkeys develop an enviable degree of agility at an early age, they remain 'babies' to their mothers for at least two years. This shows an almost human emotional dependence in the mother-child relationship of the monkey, as most other mammals cease to look after their offspring much sooner after birth.

Not all animals breed readily in captivity but the number that is doing so in zoos is increasing. The reason is that zoos are beginning to cater for

(1) Wild female rabbit; (2) baby albino rabbit; (3) pure bred black and white Dutch rabbit, pure bred blue and white Dutch rabbit, and New Zealand white rabbit; (4) orange Rex rabbit; (5) white rabbit and cinnamon rabbit; (6) cross-bred English rabbits; (7) young grey rabbit; (8) young albino rabbit; (9) white rabbit.

the environmental needs of animals. Years ago large animals were kept in unsuitable surrounding such as cages and no attempt was made to recreate any of the features present in their natural habitat. Hence the animals were disorientated and their emotional and sexual behaviour reflected their alienation from their native lands. Today more thought is given and more money spent in catering for the well-being of the large beasts such as lions, tigers, pandas, giraffes and bears. They live in much more natural surroundings which has improved their morale and they now breed successfully.

Play

The more intelligent of the mammals, once they get past the purely sleeping and suckling routine, develop an insatiable need to play. Looking funny and adorable as they do, it is hard to imagine that their playing has any other significance than mere youthful exuberance and sheer enjoyment of life. That element obviously exists but it is not the central purpose and the type and quality of play is not just arbitrary. Playing for all young mammals has a serious underlying purpose. It is an essential developmental factor at a particular stage of growth. In human terms and to coin a psychological phrase, play is "the work of the child."

It has a twofold purpose. The first is to practise and develop physical skills and the second is as a preparation for life. In the same way as for the human child, a baby animal needs to play to test its strength against the realities of the world outside. It needs to know that its limbs and its senses are responding correctly to the stimuli it receives. At first the young mammal starts to play in the comfortable proximity of its mother's accepting warmth. It tries to pit its strength against her own, knowing that no harm will come to it. Observation of all species of mammals teaches us that mothers not only tolerate but encourage these

(1) Asian tree frog; (2) and (9) tortoise; (3), (4) and (7) common frog; (5) European tree frog; (6) green toad; (8) hedgehog.

6

7

8

9

playful attempts by their offspring, even to the point of harassment. Watching a lioness can be a real education in this area. A patient lioness will put up with endless torment from her cubs, even while she is trying to snatch a moment's sleep between her heavy nursing duties. Suddenly, with one cuff, she will swipe them all into momentary submission to show them who is the boss.

As the young mammals grow more mature they will be encouraged by the mother to venture out further. She will initiate situations which prepare her offspring for life without her. For example all members of the cat family will bring in live prey and then stand back and watch the babies trying to deal with the situation with occasional prompts and training tips that they can imitate. These role playing situations are set up from very early on at regular sessions and in growing degrees of difficulty.

Animals know how to pace their teaching situation to coincide with their offspring's rate of readiness.

Play varies according to the life style of the particular species of mammal. Animals who hunt for their food play predatory games; ones that involve stalking and speedy attacks. Animals who are frequently hunted play games of escapes from attacks, listening and recognising dangers, learning how to follow the herd leader and stick close to an escaping herd as well as defensive tactics for when attacks take place. Each species, through play, practices strategies for the particular roles they are to play in life. It is instinctive behaviour on their part and perhaps also to do with the ancestral memory that all mammal

babies possess, as well as the ability to imitate their parents, which makes them learn so quickly and know what to do and how to play. Evidence shows that a great deal of animal behaviour is due to an inbuilt mechanism inherent in the animal at birth and not merely conditioning which teaches the young to learn so quickly.

It has been suggested, and there is plenty of evidence that this is so, that human children who are deprived of natural forms of play when very young develop all sorts of inhibitions and learning problems at a later stage. There is no reason why this theory should not apply to animals too. In the most unlikely situation that a kitten, cub or pup might be deprived of play, they would turn out to be very unconfident creatures.

Communication

When considering how animals communicate we have to eradicate from our minds the notion of language. Language is a system of symbols unique to man. Because humans are also mammals we share some of the non-verbal signals that animals use to communicate with each other, but we as a species are alone in having produced a system which communicates in symbolic terms. This is why language is sometimes a barrier as well as an advantage in human communication. It forces us to learn the exact symbols in order to communicate with members of the same species in different parts of the world.

Animals employ a system of communication which relates to their environment. Sounds are used as opposed to words and these express emotional attitudes and responses to situations. Certainly mammals speak to their young and to each other by using tonal expression in conjunction with bodily postures. Cats hiss and crouch in a springing position to indicate aggression towards an unwanted situation. They purr and recline comfortably to indicate

*(1) Arab mare and foal; (2) young donkey and mother;
(3) grey mare and foal; (4) chestnut mare and foal;
(5) palomino mare and chestnut foal; (6) Arab foal;
(7) and (8) donkeys with their offspring.*

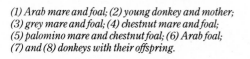

6

7

8

1

2

3

4

5

6

pleasure and ease. All mammals including humans use tone to communicate with each other. They coo and make loving noises to their young and make whimpering noises when unhappy or afraid.

Acoustic signals are common too. They do not require the visual element of seeing the body posture. Alarm cries from a distance to express warning or to locate lost members of a family or a herd can be communicated effectively by members of the same species. Acoustic signals are sometimes not even distinguishable to the ears of humans or other species of mammals. Gerbils commonly produce ultrasonic squeaks.

Chemical signals or pheromones are important in the social behaviour of many animals. A scent trail exuded by a courting mammal will immediately alert its mate and convey a precise message.

Another form of communication employed by mammals is the 'sign stimulus.' This is purely how an animal looks or what its behaviour implies. A baboon standing upright, puffing out its chest, beating it and advancing towards another male is using pure body language to imply that it is the master here and prepared to prove it. Other forms of 'sign stimuli' are used in mating – all mammals express messages about their feelings by the way they look and behave to suggest attraction, acquiescence or rejection.

Animals' communication with their offspring is largely dependent on smell signals. It is based on recognition of distinguishing smells. Mothers frequently sniff their children to make sure they belong to them. When a sheep loses its young at birth it is often the practice to introduce a twin from another ewe within the first few hours of its abortive birth. To persuade it to adopt a lamb which is not its own, the dead lamb's skin and fleece is cut away, stripped off and wrapped tightly around the adoptive lamb's body.

(1) Arab horse and foal; (2) part-bred Arab colt; (3) Arab horse and foal; (4) part-bred Arab colt; (5) part-bred Arab mare and foal; (6) young donkey; (7) pure-bred Arab mare and foal; (8) part-bred Arab colt.

Small Animals

It seems very surprising when one thinks about it to realise how large a part small mammals have played in our lives throughout history.

Even though a greater number of people in the western world live in cities and work in urban conditions compared with those who work on the land, small animals, even if they only exist for most people in picture books, television or Walt Disney cartoons, still play a vital part in nature and in people's lives.

Human beings are interested in animals. They need to relate to them because they are in danger of losing touch with nature and because they are a constant reminder of the animal element in themselves. Often we do not see animals as they really are but as sweet furry creatures with slightly human characters; cuddly, lovable beings with all the qualities we would like to possess and none of our vices. The more we are removed from the animal environment, the more we view them in a sentimental fashion. Fed on a diet of Beatrix Potter, Kenneth Grahame and numerous

(1) Part-bred Arab colt; (2) palomino mare and foals; (3) chestnut mare and foal; (4) donkey and foal; (5) heavy horse and foal; (6) donkey and foal.

other writings for children about animals, it is not surprising that we are sentimental. Many a vegetarian is born, not because of an intrinsic dislike of the taste of flesh or for purely nutritional reasons, but from a revulsion at the thought of eating Percy the pet rabbit or Thomasina the family duck.

4

5

6

Childrens' literature is partly responsible for humanising and sentimentalising small animals – in reality these feelings are only skin deep. The scuttling mouse which suddenly hurtles across the kitchen floor sending the woman of the house screaming onto the nearest chair, is not the darling little comic from Walt Disney anymore. We quickly revert to our basic natures and attitudes as we rush to the nearest hardware store for neat little traps or poison.

Only an affluent society keeps animals as pets. In fact, the keeping of pets is historically fairly recent. Until the last century small animals were either in the wild state, or if tamed by man, they were at least kept as a useful commodity. The cat kept the mice at bay, dogs killed rats, rounded up sheep, helped man in the pursuit of game and in the control of vermin; their duties even today, in two-thirds of the world.

Today the pet is a friend of man. It helps to ward off loneliness in old people. It is a family friend, useful for teaching children to care, entertaining and loved for no utilitarian purpose but, rather, because it is furry, loveable and good.

Today the pet population is not confined to small dogs, cats, birds and fish. An enormous number of small animals find their way into the home to share family life. Most small pet owners are children, who form strong attachments to animals from a very early age.

One of the most popular pets is the Guinea pig. Originating way back from South America, the Guinea pig has been a domestic pet in Europe since the 16th century. It is a docile little rodent that gnaws its way through mounds of nuts and paper and into children's hearts. The Guinea pig is not difficult to keep in good health and is inexpensive to feed.

Other favourite pets are hamsters that originated from Germany and parts of Asia. These cartoon-like creatures with their pouchy cheeks are nocturnals and therefore most active when their owners are asleep.

Farmyard animals hold a special appeal for children – gambolling lambs and kids frolick in the green fields, while young calves capture the hearts of all who see them.

1

2

3

4

5

6

8

9

10

Delightful as they look, they can be extremely aggressive, particularly the males, and in farming areas are not regarded with sentimental affection but as destructive pests best exterminated.

Other pets kept in great numbers are gerbils, small, soft, fawn coloured rodents who spend most of their lives out of sight in the depths of the sawdust they are kept in. These too originate from Asia and reproduce at such speed that two gerbils turn into twenty at the wink of an eye.

11

(1),(4) and (10) Young lambs with their mothers; (2) goats and their offspring; (3) and (11) lambs can be marked in a variety of ways; (5) sow and her large litter; (6),(7) and (9) calves; (8) kids.

Mice are very popular pets with children – though not generally with their mothers! Fancy varieties are available as pets with various colours and markings which are not usually seen on the common mouse of the field or kitchen type. These creatures are gentle and tame easily and are often to be found up little boys' sleeves, as are their cousins the rats, of which enthusiasts have bred some spectacular varieties bearing no resemblance to the sleazy sewer rat that spreads disease.

Apart from the well known species there has recently been a demand for the more exotic animals for domestic pets, and those who trade in them have been only too ready to supply this by importing small animals from all parts of the world, many of whom would much rather have been left in their native lands.

Small monkeys have their attractions for some people, because of their imitative abilities and endearing ways, but it is difficult to

imagine the satisfaction of keeping these extremely active animals domestically. They require such special handling if they are not to end up sick and miserable through lack of exercise, incorrect diet and unsuitable living conditions. The best place for exotic animals, other than their natural habitat, is the zoo where expert attention and more suitable surroundings can be provided.

There are few small animals which are considered wild. Some people have attempted to keep certain small wild animals as pets. These include foxes being kept as dogs and efforts have been made to domesticate such unlikely subjects as otters and badgers. Only experts such as Williamson, Maxwell and Lorenz have succeeded where others have failed, because of their deep under-standing of the habits of the animals they were dealing with.

The survival of small animals in Britain is a fascinating study. The dog is probably the earliest domesticated animal in Europe and is now unimaginable as a feral species. It is now the closest to and most loved animal by man. Dogs as opposed to most other animals are probably capable of the greatest display of devotion towards man. One of the most interesting features of this species is the enormous variety in colour shape and size.

Cats are fascinating pets. Enigmatic creatures, it is often said that they are not truly domesticated animals but rather "A wild animal which has chosen to live in a house." They are fiercely independent and capable of survival in the wild without too much difficulty.

Small animals in a wild state seem to survive better in colonies than on their own. The success of the mouse and the rat seems to point to this. Both of these species seem to thrive in human environments and in urban conditions.

The rat originated in central Asia but is now a citizen of everywhere in the world. First to arrive in Europe in the 14th century was the black rat

Big cat cubs can make the best of friends, as these pictures (1), (2) and (3) show. Beautifully-marked are the tiger cubs pictured here (4), (5) and (7), while the lion cub (6) displays markings which will reduce in later life.

(Rattus Rattus) bringing with it bubonic plague – the Black Death. In the 18th century the Brown Rat (Rattus Norvegicus) appeared on the scene, an aggressive type which has more or less superseded his black brother.

Apart from the danger the rat poses to our health by being such an effective carrier of disease, this large population of predators destroys millions of tons of food-stuffs each year. Chemical rat control has been successful in keeping down the problem to manageable proportions but recently a sinister development has occurred. Many rats have become resistant to Warfarin, the main chemical agent used to exterminate them. Not only has this increased the rat population but it is said that it has produced bigger and better rats.

A similar situation has occurred with the rabbit population. Some years ago, alarmed by the growing numbers of rabbits destroying farmer's crops, myxomatosis was artificially introduced as a pest control, and it virtually wiped out the rabbit population. In recent years the rabbit has made a comeback and seems to be more or less resistant to myxomatosis. It has changed its living habits to a certain extent, especially in woodland areas, living much more above the ground than in the past. It is strange to think that both these species, the rat and the rabbit, made memorable in such literary master-pieces as "The Wind in the Willows" and "Watership Down," are such dangers to the human world.

The hare, though closely related to the rabbit, being of the same family –Leporidae–differs physically from the rabbit in several ways; chiefly the formation of the hind legs which are extremely long and much stronger making hares far speedier animals. Their living habits are dissimilar too. Unlike the rabbits who live communally in underground colonies, the hare is a solitary animal who lives wholly above the ground in open country. It constructs open nest-like "forms" in the grass. Compared

Members of the cat family look cute and cuddly, particularly when young, but they are always dangerous and unpredictable.

with the rabbit population, the hare is scarce. It breeds less frequently than the rabbit who often produces eight litters of up to nine young in a year.

The hare also attracts the attention of the blood sports enthusiasts who course it with greyhounds and hunt it with harriers. The hare is much more in danger of extinction than the rabbit but it is ingenious and adaptable. It can now be found on the vast grassy stretches between the runways at Heathrow and other airports.

Another small animal which man persecutes is the fox. A beautiful animal and the subject of many stories in literature (la Fontaine, Aesop) it has the reputation of being cunning. The fox too is considered a pest in rural areas as it is very partial to poultry and one fox can cause

(1) Kangaroo and pouched baby; (2) giraffes; (3) zebras; (4) and (8) bison; (5), (6) and (10) elephants–the size of their ears indicates their African origin; (7) deer; (9) grey seal pup; (11) short-clawed otter.

havoc and total destruction not only to a poultry farm but to a whole area.

In many areas of the countryside the fox is protected from the traps and the guns of the poultry keepers so that it may be hunted for sport by hounds and in England alone there are at least two hundred packs of foxhounds. The fox breeds only once a year, producing litters of 5 to 8 young in April. The young cubs reach maturity in eighteen months. The fox is a born survivor. It adapts well to circumstances and since the shortage of rabbits, one of its prime sources of food, it has moved into more suburban areas where it has become extremely adept at scavenging from dustbins and rubbish dumps.

9

10

8

11

1

2

3

5

6

4

7

One small animal which is now under pressure from humans is the badger, which is a true inhabitant of the countryside. It is not often seen because it is a nocturnal animal. During the daylight hours it spends its time in a burrow or sett. A beautiful animal, with its distinctive black and white markings, its food is mainly grubs and insects, but it is quite omnivorous too, eating also vegetables, shoots and bark. Until recently badgers were also hunted for pleasure by humans with dogs, but pressures applied by animal preservation societies on the grounds that its survival was at risk saved it from possible extinction.

Lately however, it has been suggested that the badger is a carrier of bovine tuberculosis and therefore a dangerous animal and steps are being taken once again to reduce the badger population in parts of the country.

A proliferous small animal which is very much a part of the English scene is the squirrel. Definitely a favourite in children's literature and art, Squirrel Nutkin from Beatrix Potter has influenced many a small child's view of what, apart from its luxurious tail, is very much a member of the "Rattus" family. It too is considered a pest because of its habit of destroying the bark of trees in forests. The traditional red squirrel in England was virtually driven out by the grey squirrel which was introduced from Canada. A very adaptable animal and a strong survivor, the grey squirrel seems to multiply and colonise even in parks in the heart of big cities. They are not timid considering their wild state and are known to have "harassed" housewives at the doors and windowsills of urban homes. They are certainly not an animal in danger of extinction.

Town dwellers are, on the whole, deprived of day to day contact with small wild animals, apart from the squirrels which they might see in their back gardens, the unwanted mouse and the occasional hedgehog or rabbit which can be seen in the

9

(1) Horned oryx and family; (2) llama and offspring; (3) rhino and baby; (4) red panda cub; (5) baboons and their young; (6) young koala bear; (7) fox cub; (8) and (9) polar bear cub.

1

2

3

4

5

7

hedgerows. Generally it is through television programmes and picture books that urban people are kept aware of the vast varieties of species in the animal world.

Really the best place to see small animals in all their variety is in a good zoo, something which every big city has. They are especially suitable for displaying small animals, because unlike the varieties of large wild animals where removal from their natural habitat poses controversial arguments about whether it is cruel to keep lions or bears in cages, a small

11

(1) Penguins; (2) red panda cub; (3) baby giraffe; (4) young deer; (5) chimpanzee; (6) and (8) horned oryx family; (7) and (10) zebra; (9) llama; (11) koala bear and baby.

10

animal's environment can be created successfully in zoos so that they feel quite at home. Complete sections in zoos are devoted to nocturnal animals, where by means of artificial light changes, day is turned into night and we can observe the activities of creatures which would be impossible in normal circumstances.

The idea of a zoo is basically educational both for the public and for those engaged in research on all aspects of animal life, and of course it is a way of preventing the extinction of certain species.

First English edition published in 1981 by Colour Library International Ltd.
This edition is published by Crescent Books, Distributed by Crown Publishers Inc.
Illustrations and text © : Colour Library International Ltd. 163 East 64th Street, New York 10021.
Colour separations by FERCROM, Barcelona, Spain.
Display and text filmsetting by Focus Photoset, London, England.
Printed by Cayfosa and bound by Eurobinder - Barcelona (Spain)
All rights reserved.
Library of Congress Catalog Card Number: 81-67588
CRESCENT 1981

Dep. Leg. B. 3.124/82